Let's Get Ready for Valentine's Day

By Lloyd G. Douglas

Welcome Books™

Children's Press®
A Division of Scholastic Inc.
New York / Toronto / London / Auckland / Sydney
Mexico City / New Delhi / Hong Kong
Danbury, Connecticut

Thanks to the Tick Tock Early Learning Center in Avondale, PA

Photo Credits: Cover and all photos by Maura B. McConnell
Contributing Editor: Jennifer Silate
Book Design: Daniel Hosek

Library of Congress Cataloging-in-Publication Data

Douglas, Lloyd G.
  Let's get ready for Valentine's Day / by Lloyd G. Douglas.
  p. cm. -- (Celebrations)
  Includes index.
  Summary: A young girl describes ways that she celebrates Valentine's day
  at school and at home.
  ISBN 0-516-24261-X (lib. bdg.) -- ISBN 0-516-24353-5 (pbk.)
  1. Valentine's Day--Juvenile literature. [1. Valentine's Day. 2.
  Holidays.] I. Title. II. Celebrations (Children's Press)

GT4925 .D68 2003
394.2618--dc21

2002007132

Contents

My name is Katie.

Tomorrow is **Valentine's Day**.

5

My class is getting ready.

My teacher tells us that on Valentine's Day, we **celebrate** love.

We are making cards for
Valentine's Day.

I am going to make a card
for my mom and dad.

9

I use a red **crayon** to draw on my card.

I draw hearts on my card.

11

I also write "Happy Valentine's Day" on my card.

13

Look at the **calendar**.

It is February 14.

We celebrate Valentine's Day on February 14.

When I get home from school, my parents give me a Valentine's Day card.

17

I give my card to
my parents.

They like it a lot.

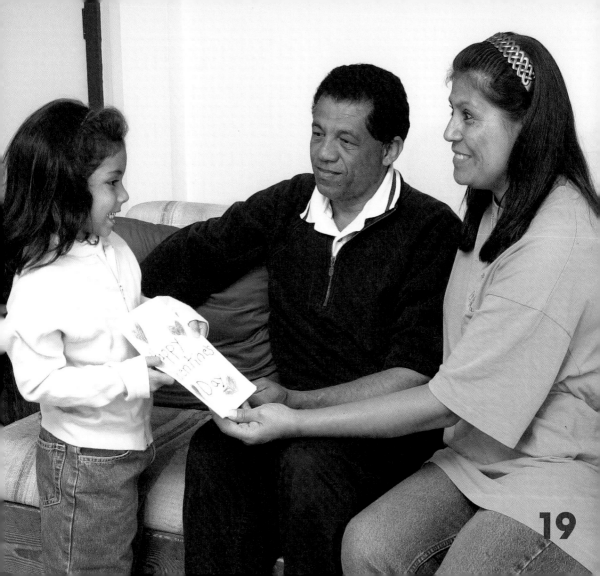

Happy Valentine's Day!

New Words

calendar (**kal**-uhn-dur) a chart showing all the days, weeks, and months in a year

celebrate (**sel**-uh-brate) to do something enjoyable on a special occasion

crayon (**kray**-uhn) a colored wax stick used for drawing and coloring

Valentine's Day (**val**-uhn-tinez **day**) February 14, a day named in honor of Saint Valentine; it is celebrated by sending cards

To Find Out More

Books
The Story of Valentine's Day
by Clyde Robert Bulla
HarperCollins Children's Books

Valentine's Day
by David F. Marx
Children's Press

Web Site
Valentine Fun at Kids Domain
http://www.kidsdomain.com/holiday/val/
You can read about the history of Valentine's Day, send e-cards to
your friends, and much more on this Web site.

Index

About the Author

Lloyd G. Douglas is an editor and writer of children's books.

Reading Consultants

Kris Flynn, Coordinator, Small School District Literacy, The San Diego County Office of Education

Shelly Forys, Certified Reading Recovery Specialist, W.J. Zahnow Elementary School, Waterloo, IL

Sue McAdams, Former President of the North Texas Reading Council of the IRA, and Early Literacy Consultant, Dallas, TX